AF375228

15 - 2 = 13
3 - 1 = 2

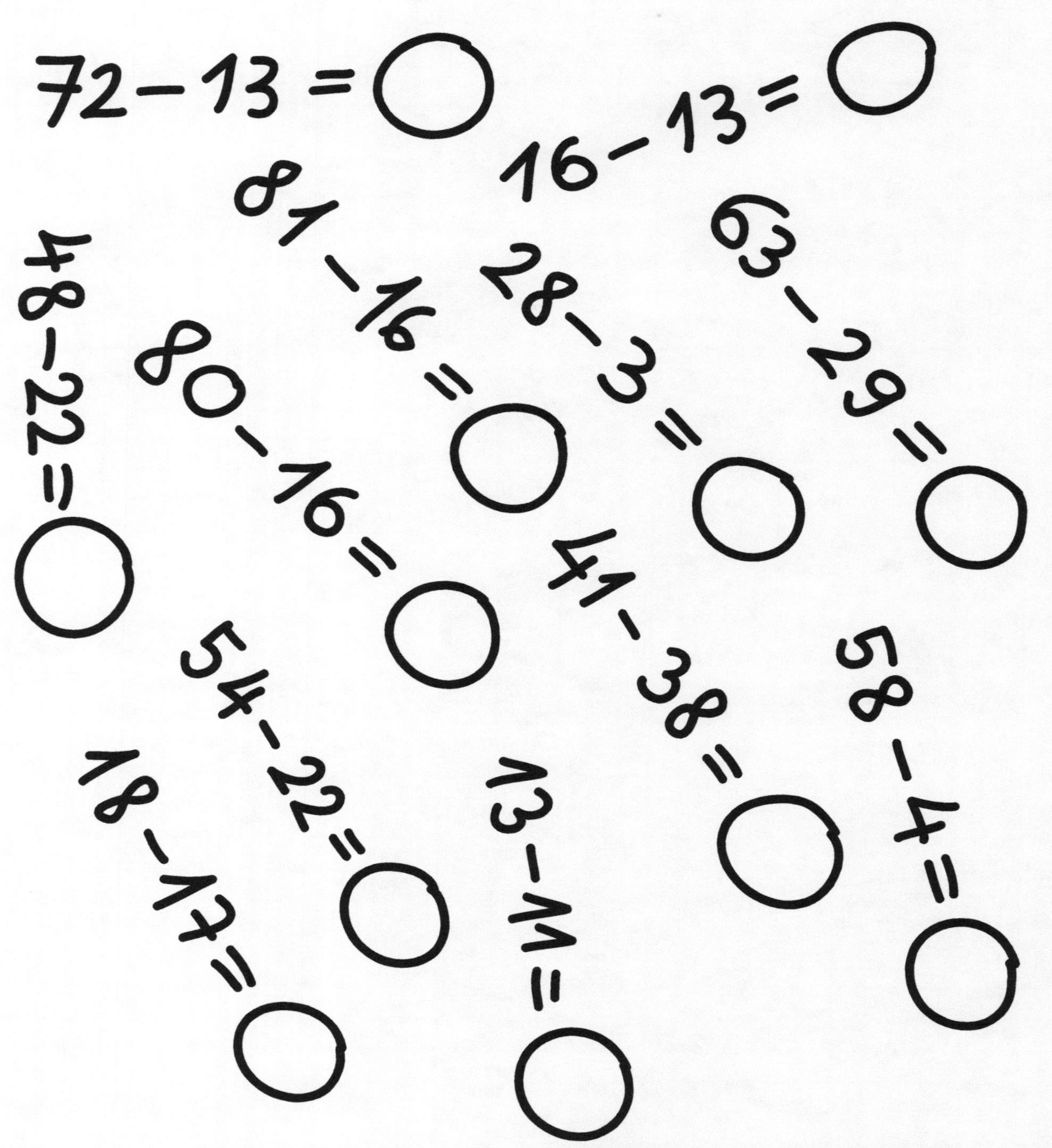

72 - 13 =
16 - 13 =
81 - 16 =
28 - 3 =
63 - 29 =
48 - 22 =
80 - 16 =
41 - 38 =
58 - 4 =
54 - 22 =
13 - 11 =
18 - 17 =

16-13=○

23-6=○

32-2=○

82-21=○

12-8=○

74-32=○

44-1=○

23-11=○

24-5=○

26-3=○

88-45=○

93-20=○

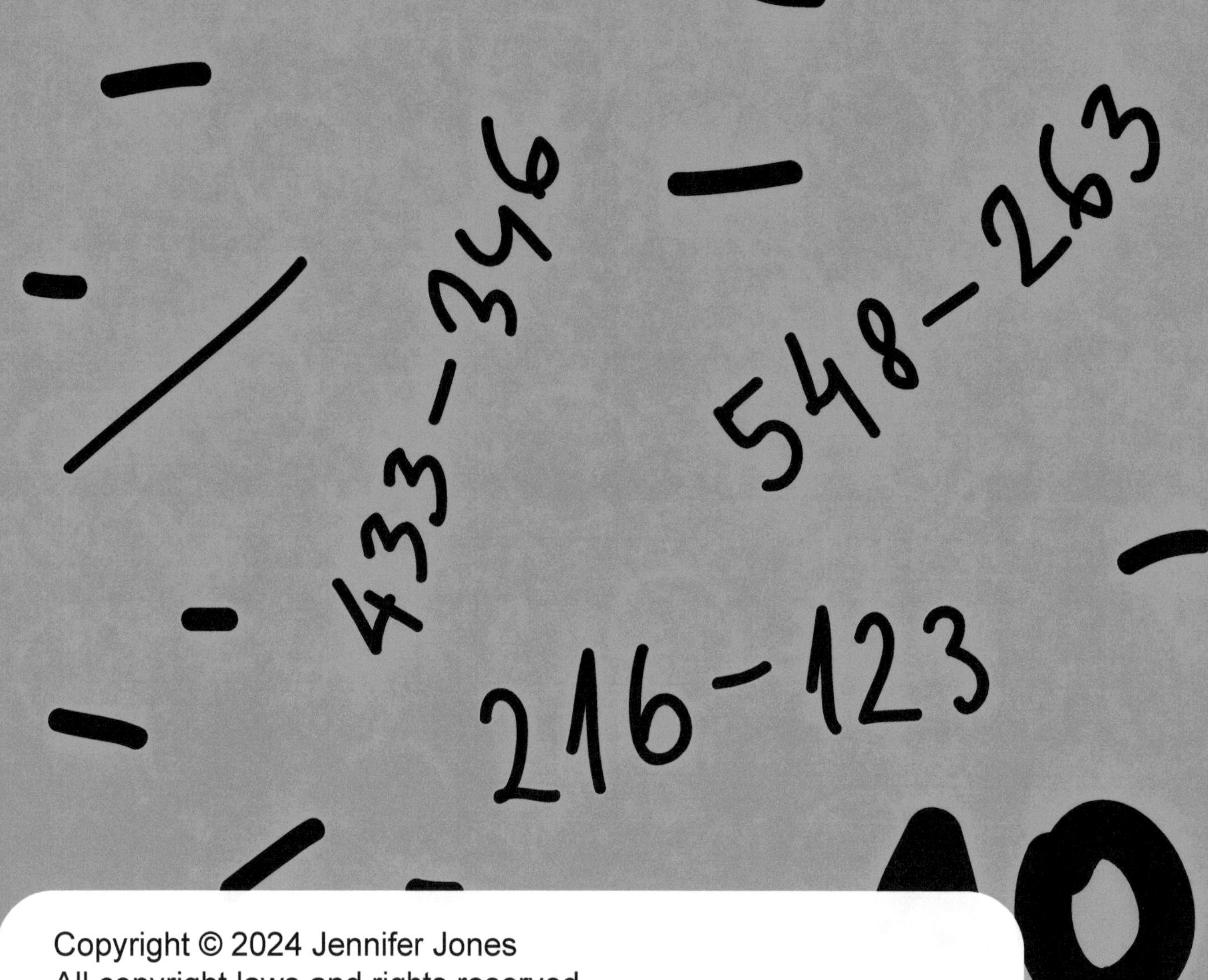

Linus the Minus

A Subtraction Adventure

By Jennifer Jones

In a classroom full of noisy cheer,
The teacher sighed, "I need an aid!"
Then came Linus the Minus,
"I'll help students make the grade!"

13-5
5-3

Linus grinned as he struck a pose,
"Math is magic—you'll see it's true!
Just subtract to find what's left.
It's easy, and I'll show you how to!"

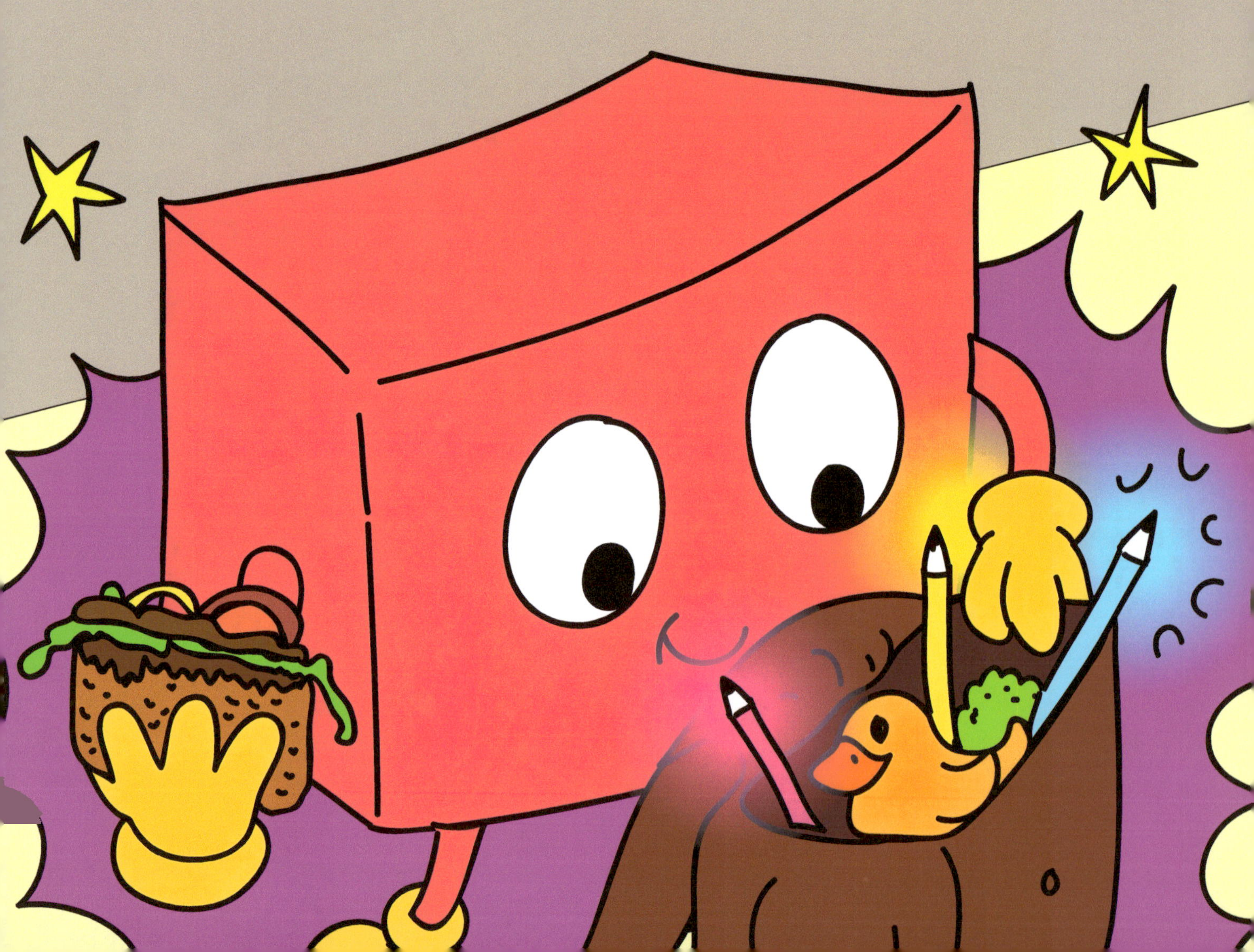

The kids were curious, so he began,
"Here's a pile of blocks, let's take away three."
From twelve to nine with a swift swipe,
"Subtract, and see what's left for me!"

12-3=?

But as Linus showed his subtraction flair,
He snatched two markers with a cheeky grin.
"You had five markers, now there's three!"
The kids all shouted, "That's a sin!"

SUBTRACTION WIZARD?

Linus tripped and the blocks went flying,
He laughed, "Subtraction isn't my friend!"
The class jumped in to help him out,
And solved the mess together in the end.

YOU SUBTRACTED YOURSELF!

"Let's try again," Linus said with a grin,
"Start with twelve apples and take away five."
A student called out, "The answer is seven!"
Linus beamed, "You're keeping math alive!"

12-5= 7

"Six toy cars, but I'll take away one."
"Five cars left," the kids all cheered.
The teacher smiled and joined the fun,
"Subtracting's fun! It's not so weird."

6 - 1 = 5

Linus grabbed three pencils from the floor,
"You had ten; now there are seven instead!"
The students laughed and did the math,
"Let's solve more problems!" one of them said.

7 =
10 - 7 = 3
MATH ROCKS?

But Linus faced a tricky plight—
His satchel could hold twenty, not a thing more!
With six apples, three cars, five pens,
"How many more can I store?"

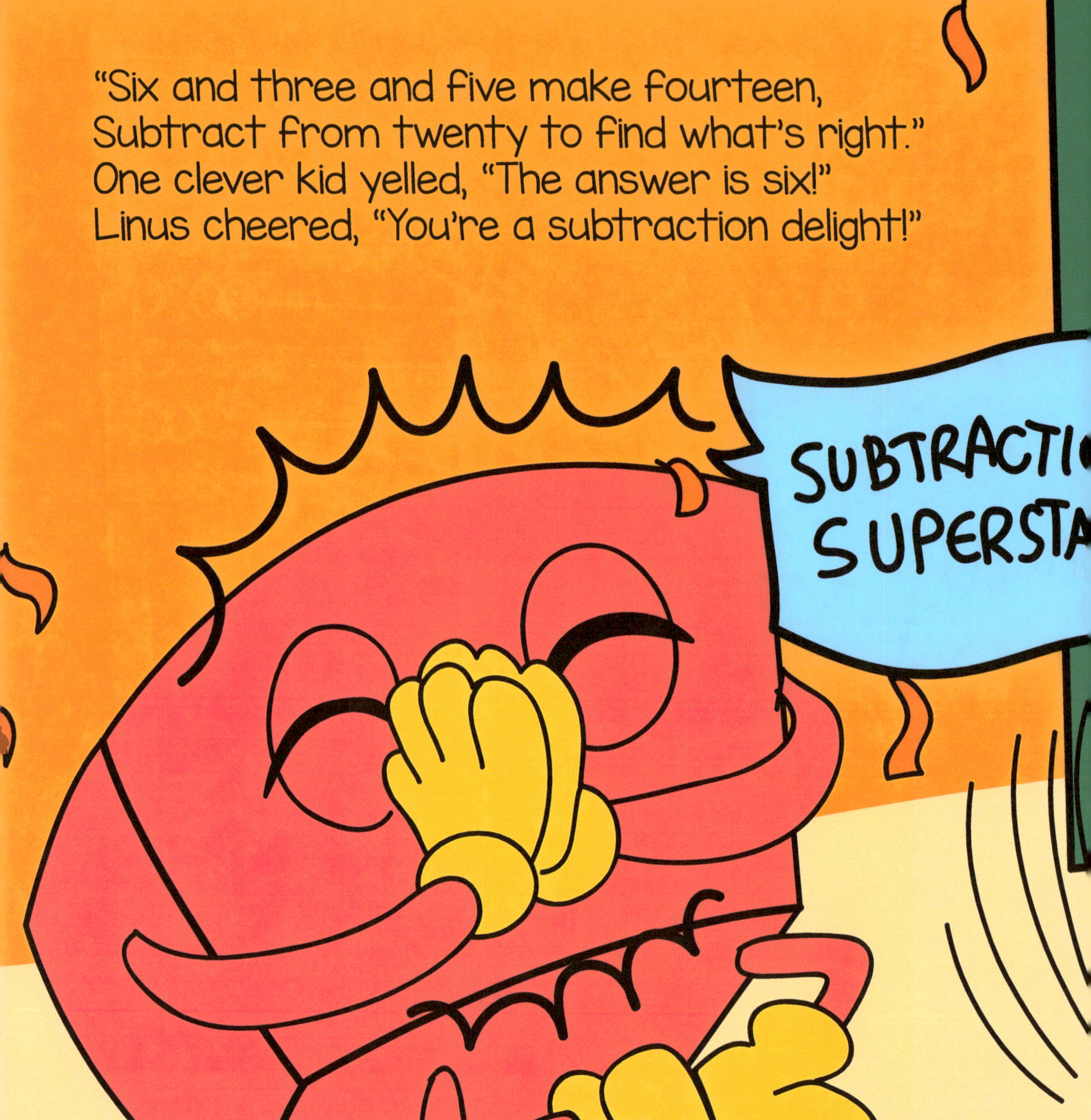

"Six and three and five make fourteen,
Subtract from twenty to find what's right."
One clever kid yelled, "The answer is six!"
Linus cheered, "You're a subtraction delight!"

20 - 14 = 6
It's 6!

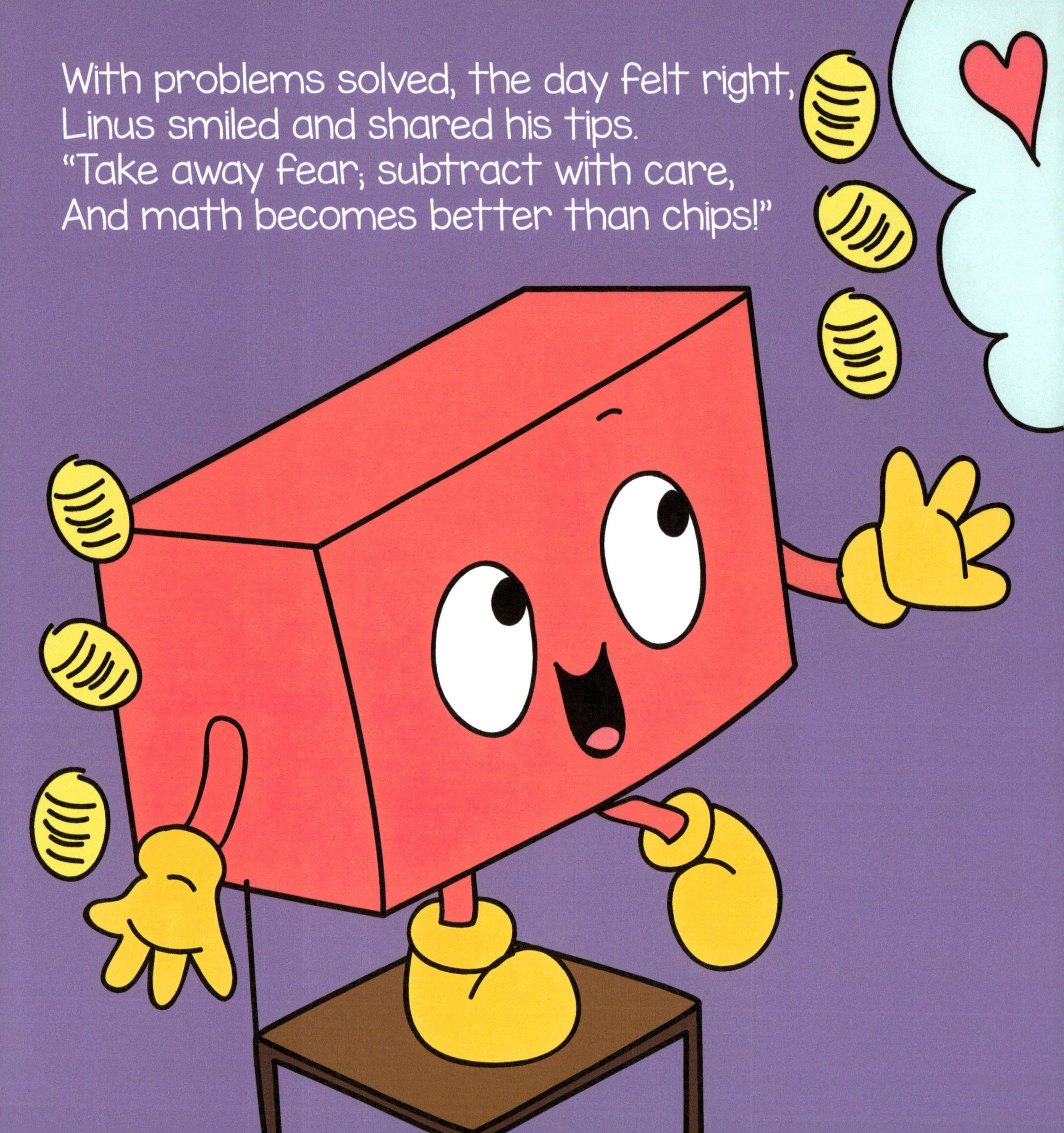

With problems solved, the day felt right,
Linus smiled and shared his tips.
"Take away fear; subtract with care,
And math becomes better than chips!"

7-4=3
6-1=5
6-
13-3
18-8=10
5-1
24-

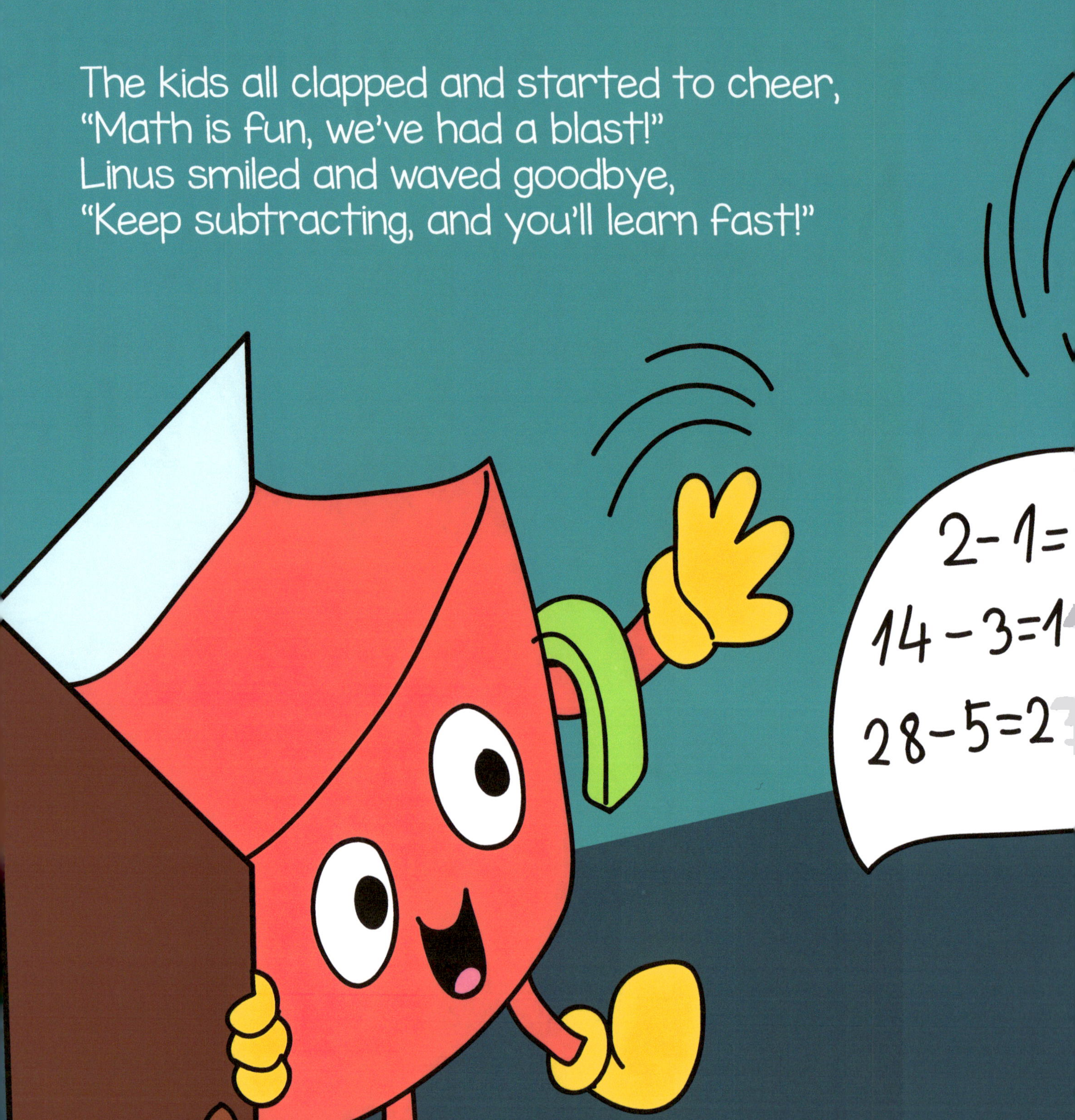

The kids all clapped and started to cheer,
"Math is fun, we've had a blast!"
Linus smiled and waved goodbye,
"Keep subtracting, and you'll learn fast!"
2 - 1 =
14 - 3 = 1
28 - 5 = 2

8 - 3 = 5
16 - 3 = 13

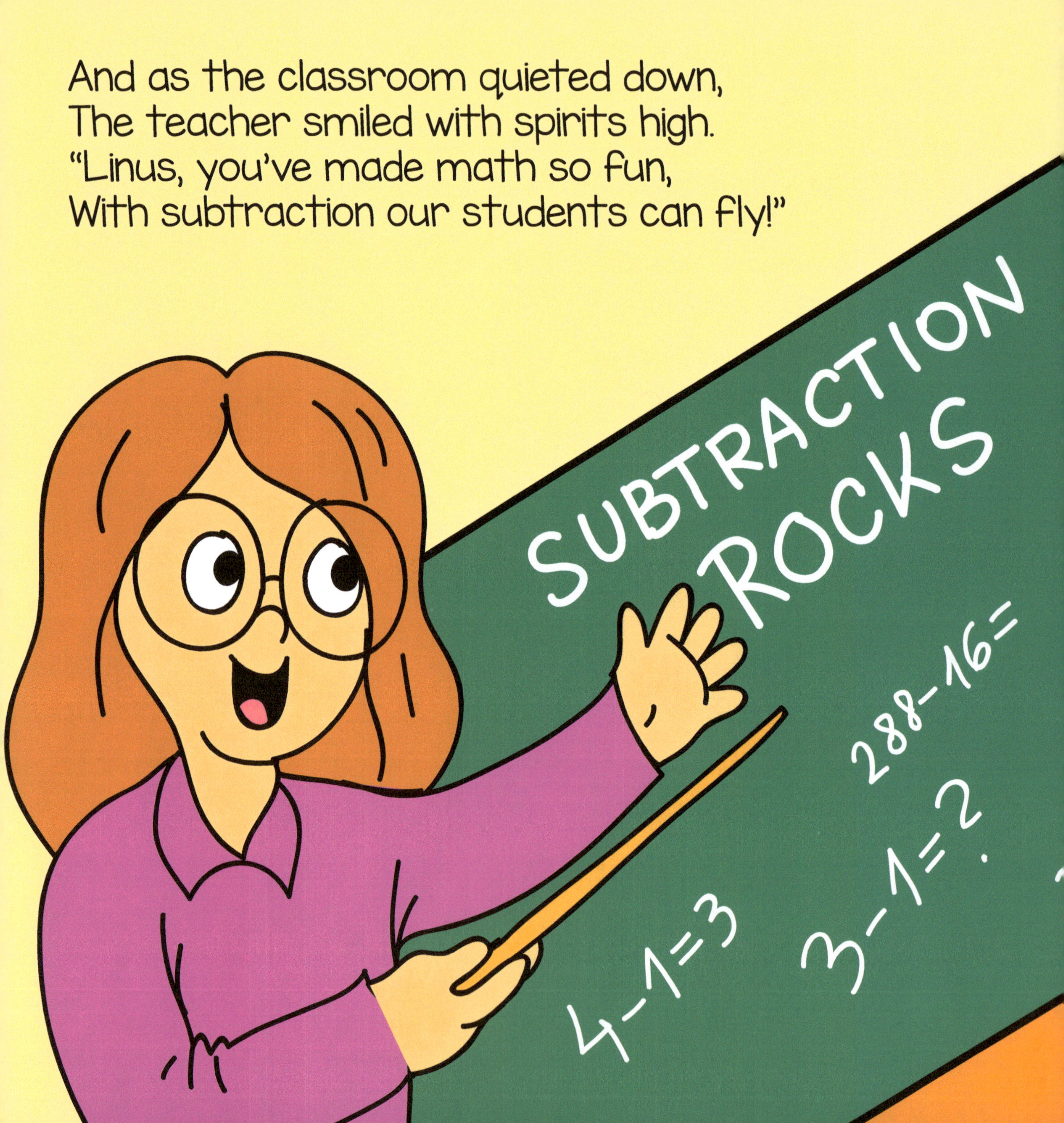

And as the classroom quieted down,
The teacher smiled with spirits high.
"Linus, you've made math so fun,
With subtraction our students can fly!"
SUBTRACTION
ROCKS
288-16=
4-1=3
3-1=2

5-4

Subtraction Scavenger Hunt

Objective: Practice subtraction through real-world objects.

How to Play:

- Kids gather items (e.g., pencils, toys, blocks).

- Each child starts with a set number of items (e.g., 10 blocks).

-A helper (or "Linus") takes away a few items from each pile.

-Kids write the subtraction problem to find out how many are left (e.g., "10 – 3 = 7").

-**Bonus**: Add a storytelling twist: "Linus needs 3 blocks to help his satchel!"

Linus's Subtraction Puzzle

Objective: Solve fun subtraction problems with illustrations from the story.

Example Puzzles:

- Linus starts with 12 apples. He gives 5 to his teacher. How many are left?
- Linus grabs 10 pencils but drops 4. How many does he have now?
- **Bonus** Challenge: Kids can draw their own subtraction problem and share it with the class.

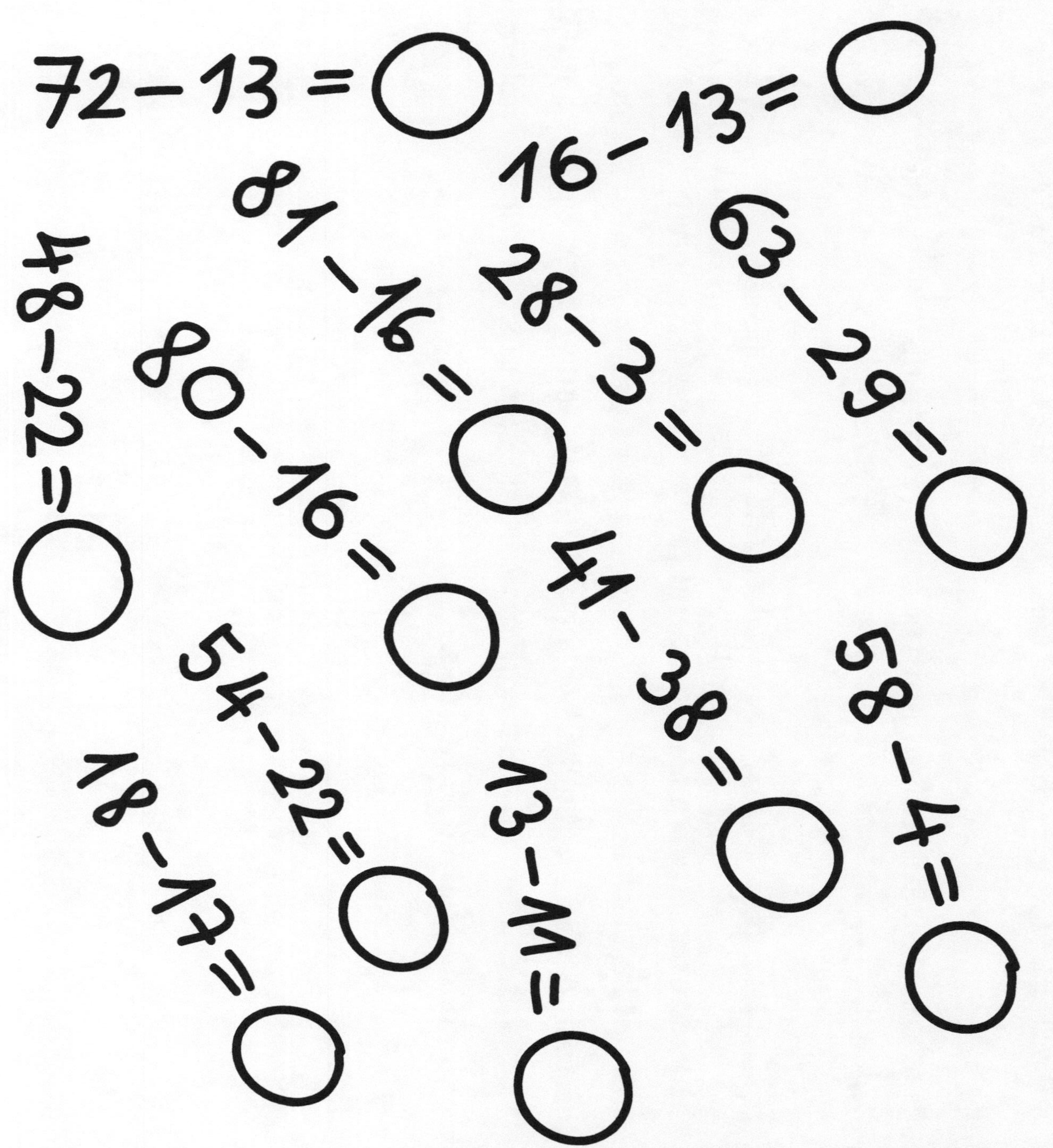

72 - 13 =
16 - 13 =
63 - 29 =
81 - 16 =
28 - 3 =
48 - 22 =
80 - 16 =
41 - 38 =
58 - 4 =
54 - 22 =
13 - 11 =
18 - 17 =

16 − 13 = ◯

23 − 6 = ◯

32 − 2 = ◯

82 − 21 = ◯

12 − 8 = ◯

74 − 32 = ◯

44 − 1 = ◯

23 − 11 = ◯

24 − 5 = ◯

26 − 3 = ◯

88 − 45 = ◯

93 − 20 = ◯